I0616174

SIX is for 6enocide

poems ▼ *reflections* ▼ *rants*

daniel s. reyes

Gaza is apocalyptic.

For the Alaydi family in Gaza, Palestine

Amna, Salem, Alma, Yamen, Ola, Rama, Laay, Haya,
Narmeen, Maye, Rolla, Noor Ah-Huda, Rana, Amal,
Shireen, Salem Mosbah, Medhat, Mosbah, Hammam

An Invitation

for the nervous system and the anxiety of watching a genocide livestreamed in 4k quality

Box Breathing Exercise
1. **Visualize**: imagine a box to guide your breath.
2. **Inhale**: breathe in slowly for a count of four, visualizing going up the first side of the box.
3. **Hold**: hold your breath for a count of four.
4. **Exhale**: exhale slowly for a count of four, visualizing going down the second side.
5. **Hold**: hold your breath again for a count of four.
6. **Repeat**: continue for several rounds.

4-7-8 Breathing
1. **Sit Comfortably**: Sit with a straight back.
2. **Inhale**: breathe in silently through your nose for a count of four.
3. **Hold**: hold your breath for a count of seven.
4. **Exhale**: exhale completely through your mouth with a "whoosh" sound for a count of eight.
5. **Repeat**: repeat the cycle up to three more times.

*please take care of yourself. seek community so you have people to talk to about what you're seeing on your phone everyday…go for walks…exercise…read…take action!

*keep in mind: Gaza doesn't have the luxury to prioritize their mental health. so use your luxury to stay in the fight.

you may be wondering why a non-Palestinian person was compelled to write a book exposing the 6enocide in Gaza, Palestine? i made this because the 6enocide in Gaza is being censored by the mainstream media, and because it's the right thing to do. i'm not saying you should write a book of poetry and reflections as well, but DO something! preferably something within your wheelhouse, because publicly speaking out against a 6enocide is already out of everyone's comfort zone. use your strengths. no one should have to do this work, but here we are. it's ALL our jobs to stop a 6enocide and the **erasure** of ANY people.

this book will be littered with ways to take action and to break your silence if you haven't condemned "Israel" or unapologetically spoken out against their crimes. maybe this is your first time hearing about the 6enocide in Gaza? welcome!

this project is my way of giving back by telling stories that otherwise wouldn't make it to your news feeds at random. and even better, you get to give back as well, because all profits from this book go directly to **the Alaydi family** who's still trying to survive the 6enocide in Gaza.

maybe you purchased this book to be a supportive friend?
or maybe you saw the title and it called out to you?
whatever the case may be, thank you for your support. thank you for being curious. this is where it all starts. curiosity mixed with good discernment, and knowing right from wrong while actively choosing to do the right thing even when doing wrong pays more. but remember, having real compassion is FREE.

i wanted to clarify before you go any further. there are no sources cited within these pages, but i do encourage you to do a little research of your own. i hope what some of these poems, reflections, and rants on Gaza can do for you is shed light on what's happening in realtime, a 6enocide.

by the way, i use the number 6 to replace the letter G in "Genocide" because for the last 2 years, Meta (Instagram), has shadowbanned all accounts exposing "Israel" of its crimes. using code by replacing letters with numbers and symbols is how we're able to circumvent the system (in some small way). that being said, Meta gave the position of 'information security' to, for lack of a better term, an ex-Israeli intelligence officer, Guy Rosen. of course their security team that collects OUR data and can take down all content that makes "Israel" look bad, is run by Mossad (Hebrew acronym for The Institute for Intelligence and Special Operations). i mean, should we really be surprised by Meta's corruptiveness? and if you know anything about the apartheid state of "Israel", they specialize in, and violate cyber surveillance laws around the globe; especially in Palestine, and including the U.S.

listen. i could go on and on about what might come off as conspiracy to some, but I won't (i wish it was conspiracy). i will leave you with this though…

when a week goes by…then a month…then a year…then 2 years…and everyday and every hour all you've seen are videos on social media of children and their families being murdered and entire neighborhoods desolated by the very weapons manufactured and shipped off by the country you live in and were made using your tax dollars, you do what any sane, scrupulous person would do, start digging. i understand we are all consumed by this capitalistic world of trying to make ends meet, or for the majority of us, trying to survive instead of live. so i get that many of us would rather spend whatever little free time we have, doing something enjoyable. and to keep it **100**, mainstream media will not show you the reality of the 6enocide. they too are bought and infiltrated by "Israel".

a final thought for the faithful…

if you practice any spirit based faith or religion, i invite you to envision these questions wholeheartedly:

1. regardless of what mainstream media tells you, is killing mass amounts of people, or even killing a single person wrong? (according to your beliefs)
2. does anything justify killing someone? (according to your beliefs)
3. does your holy book tell you it's okay to murder?
4. do you pray for something and expect it to fall into place, or does prayer need to be nurtured?

END of INTRO

*- for my dear friend, **Dr. Rolla Alaydi** (over 200 family members martyred by "Israel" since October 7)*

have you ever felt shamed out of mourning the mass murder of your loved ones?

every night, you stay awake past God's bedtime praying he saves your family. but because he was at rest when you sent your prayers, you wake up the next morning, a new family member murdered.

and not only was it family, it was 60 others: men, women, children. **they all had names**. they were all made of the same God-like magic each and every human was born with. the only difference is, they were born in Palestine. they were born into a life of oppression without any say. and some were born directly into the ongoing 6enocide we're still watching on our phones, today.

so you drag yourself to work, in a way you've never done before, and you hold it "together". do not disturb or distract your colleagues with your problems, because in THIS country, your people, your family, are now widely considered subhuman, terrorists, and animals (including the children).

so the question is no longer, who would believe you? you're now faced with the question of, who would care?

it's been 686 days at the time of writing this, and the 6enocide of Palestinians in Gaza has yet to shake the world.

we have grown comfortable in our complicity, with the luxury to do nothing. but i hope these words will wake you

before the rest of Rolla's family is martyred. **pray for Gaza**.

in a perfect world

the good guys would be casted as follows: Mark Zuckerberg, Elon Musk, Jeff Bezos, Donald J. Trump, Joe Biden, Benjamin Netanyahu, Dwayne Johnson, Pharrell Williams, Taylor Swift, Beyonce Knowles, Gal Gadot…the list goes on.

but what do they all have in common besides being household names, and most of them billionaires?

they all believe that the Palestinian household and land belong to the fictional state self-proclaimed as, "Israel".
a white European lie that started over 100 years ago giving rise to the Zionist project to steal the land of Palestine in 1948 and make it a white Jewish "safe haven".

history did **NOT** start on October 7, 2023.

~~Google~~: **Nakba** (but also, **fuuuuuuuck** Google)
~~Google~~: Project Nimbus (good reason to axe google from your life)
~~Google~~: **Zionism** (Theodor Herzl)
~~Google~~: *Hind Rajab (*6-year-old Palestinian girl)
~~Google~~: **the Great March of Return**

*IOF is the acronym for "Israeli" Occupation Forces (they're actually called IDF or "Israeli" "Defense" Forces but you can't be in "defense" as the illegal occupier).
*you'll notice i put "Israel" in quotation marks all throughout this book. this signifies that "Israel" is not a real place. it is occupying the stolen land of Palestine. therefore, it is fictional whether it says "Israel" on your Google maps or not. #isnotreal

it's funny how the world works
we try to alleviate the suffering by
planning getaways and family gatherings
only to come back home in the same if not worse
misery we left with. not knowing how to truly
cope or heal. this is not your fault. there is
a system in place that puts us on a time crunch

get a college degree. a career. buy a house. get married.
have kids. retire. die. (in that order)

a checklist of things leading up to our grand exit from
this world, and we're supposed to believe that the
systems in place were designed for us to reach this seemingly
one-size-fits-all trajectory of a perfect life.
and as the story goes, the older generation makes the lives of the
younger generation more difficult to succeed, even
if they believe their method of raising their kids was the right
way (they were likely stifled by the systems in place as well).
maybe it's the American way, to abandon loved ones on our
nonstop journey attempting to attain an unrealistic list of life
goals we're expected to struggle for. it's likely a reason one of
the most common regrets people have before they die is working
too much and not making time for loved ones. the "American
Dream" is practically impossible to make a reality. i hope the
aspirations of this checklist never impede on your morality (i
know. easier said than done). trial and error until death do us
part; but at the end of the day, being in service is truly the only
thing that matters…and it's becoming a dying art.

it makes you wonder what you're willing to give up in the act of being selfless? can a college degree be put on hold for a greater cause, or be used for a greater cause? can that cup of coffee be bought with moral codes? or will we continue to watch people who have been stifled by the system, suffer for our selfishness?

to all the students out there, is your University investing in weapon manufacturing, and why? will you organize a revolution to end these investments? or will you remain complicit? is it more important to find a secure job after school knowing that job will not hire you because you're anti-genocide, anti-holocaust? did you know that while you were earning an almost useless degree, "Israel" was destroying every University in Gaza, killing medical students, aspiring teachers, engineers, journalists, artists, scientists, anyone who arms themselves with knowledge including little kids who want to become doctors knowing their families are constantly being sent to the hospital because of the "Israeli" Occupations crimes, daily?

Palestine
is no longer Palestine
because of the Zionist Project
drafted in 1897 and the British Empire (the Balfour Declaration)
pre-Holocaust meaning it was the Ashke**nazi** Jew, Theodor Herzl, planning to steal Palestine long before the **nazi**'s holocaust.

i wake up and peel my body from the mattress
but have yet to peel my eyes from the livestreamed 6enocide

there is sunlight in my room
but the world is dark

i don't know where to start
but consider this book an entire text message
from me to you
how will you respond?

… (incoming)

coffee mixed with e**mot**ions
you switch to decaf, because watching a 6enocide on your phone
for 700 days becomes the espresso shot
then when decaf gets too strong, you switch to instant
instant like death by drone strike
Switchblade 600's from Arlington, Virginia
that sweet kami**kaz**e effect they give it
just ripe to leave a newborn's body pomegranate peeled
now, if we could just find a professional fruit photographer
who also specializes in running through rubble
with never enough time to grab their cape

flashdrive:

https://afsc.org/gaza-genocide-companies

i've been obsessed with the sky lately
not short of breath but a deep sigh lately
i'm not depressed i'm terrified frankly
of all the PRESS that have died taping
the stories they've been under fire making
it's dangerous to open eyes, awaking
people like you and i praying
not only for a true saving
but an end to a 6enocide maybe
and if you happen to pass this by
your view is as good as mine, blankly
staring up at the innocent sky, thinking
what if it was you and i living where
bombs fall from gods eyes? after all
who's gonna stop him from weeping?
if the world believes in a "chosen people"
born with rifles and Hitler Bibles
reading scripture scripted by Hitler
give it a title and call it, "Israel".

- the scofield reference bible

thank God there's a bible that excuses "Israel" to steal peoples land, murder
hundreds of thousands of them, finance weapons and wield them against
children, and build a society willing to wash, rinse, and repeat the savagery all
in God's name.

the only difference between
night and day
are the decisions we make

one day we preach self care
then the next we teach hate

one day we preach fresh air
then the next it's air we take
from Arab land and the displaced

there's no escape for them
but you can be the change

even if it's just the change
you were saving for a rainy day

a five a ten a twenty could go
a long way for the stomachs
that are empty because we
send bombs instead of cake

- send cake to the Alaydi family

the occupation has closed all borders
starved the people
bombed the "safe zones"
snipered babies
raped hostages
destroyed all universities
killed aid workers
killed Americans
killed doctors and journalists
lied about October 7th
set fire & bulldozed tents (with families in them)
burning & burying them alive
and you watch and I watch
but who has the gravitas to say what's real?
or do anything at all?

- but you need "Israel" to do something more extreme before you can say
anything in order not to offend them, the oppressor, who probably pays you to
stay silent. tell me. are you free?

beware of the oppressor.
they will try to convince you that a group of people
who unite to resist their occupiers, are the enemies.
but who has all the weapons and technology?
whose narrative is all over mainstream media?
is it the resistance group called Hamas?
or is it the terrorist organization called "Israel"?

- if you've ever been locked in a cage and forced to watch
relatives and close friends die, you're likely from Gaza

this isn't some f*cking Hogwarts House Sorting Quiz, these are peoples lives.
but if it was, take your wand and create justice and liberation and **end** the
occupation and the 6enocide of Gaza, Palestine…and make "Israel" Palestine
again (smh)

what do you see when you look at me?
do you see me as human?
what if i told you i'm Palestinian?
will you see me as human then?

- (PEP) Progressive Except Palestine

currying-favor to nazi zionists

i used to wonder what type of magic the universe hid?
now all that wonder has become a distraction from what our
world thinks of a Palestinian kid.

- they are a universe

carbon footprints and atomic bombs
i remember when grandma made me mow the lawn
not knowing that term meant something different to the
colonizers mom telling her children it's ok to drop bombs as long
as the world believes they're not human
and you do it every few months so the world believes it's normal
when it's time to drop more on their heads and their beds and
their cribs and their legs and their ribs and their live laugh love
signs hung above all the pots and the lids and what if we make
the lie so damn big that by the time you're reading this none of
them will exist…

- Daniella Weiss (founder of Nachala…~~Google~~ that shit!)

not c's
not sees
not seas
not seize
not cease
nazis
nazisrael

the U.S. has vetoed **SIX** ceasefire resolutions since 2023. the **6** Day ceasefire, and the 2025 ceasefire that lasted for **6** weeks, were both violated by "Israel" in less than 24-hours of being in effect. every "ceasefire" deal is performative and a distraction. they know that if they make headlines about some deal being made, people will only read the headlines, not the full story, and people will stop paying attention. naive people will read the headline and say "see! a ceasefire! they are moral. they are the good guys." then tell me something…why is it when a Palestinian person is killed you feel nothing? why do you let the word "war" influence your "morals"? is it out of convenience? hate? are you misinformed? or just racist?

there's money to be made

but I prefer the currency of love
and the fervor of being unafraid to say

free Palestine!

deep breaths and sighs
it depends on who you ask
about the prefix
A N T I

what's the first word that comes to mind?

now let's try the suffix
C I D E

does the false pretense of one give the right to commit the other?

the Americans are so obsessed with USA
yet would rather vacation in a place where
the dollar is made of gold
and the weather is amazing
they choose destinations based on lies they've been told like
come see what's awaiting
the same Americans who call other countries a shit hole until it's
time to put on
the **lei**
the **keffiyeh**
or
the **gold**

- watch the **Olympics**? so much money is spent to watch countries compete for
the MANLY-IST country in sports, even when some of these countries are
killing each other in actual wars displaying who has the most MANLY
weapons. and let's not forget the Olympic venues cost **BILLIONS** to build,
using government subsidies to foot the bill with taxpayer dollars, but we can't
build homes for the poor or stop a 6enocide. priorities **first** right? it amazes me
that this is the world we live in.

one day when life slows down
i'll ditch the keurig and replace it with these new high tech coffee
makers called a French press
i'll take the long way going half the speed limit with my hazards
blinking for all the busy bees trapped inside my rearview
i'll visit winter towns just to watch the snow fall on the shoulders
of strangers and their "emotional support" dogs
i'll retake that sewing class just to patch things up with my
ex-bestfriend for never being there when they felt depressed
i'll feed that bird and its family that routinely sings in the
background of my dreams becoming synonymous with my
subconscious fears i sometimes conquer before rolling out of bed
i'll tell the truth about all the things I write about and how they're
really just subliminal excerpts that no one is emotionally
adjusted for
and how could we be when the last one that you ignored had no
effect on how your day went, so you think

they can ignore the 6enocide but don't stop talking about Palestine. life has not
slowed down for Gaza. the bombs are getting bigger, and the land is getting
smaller, but the bodies being killed are larger because "Israel" is running out of
children to slaughter.

i know it's summer so excuse the rain
i sometimes wonder about climate change
how the earth gets warmer and we get smarter
but the only degrees that matter are the leaves that scatter and
become flame
i wonder who we blame for what comes after?
i try to remain sincere
but what good is a brain in a disaster?
catastrophic like that one episode of *how i met your mother*, or,
the bear
it chases after you when all you've done in life is play it safe
so as you sit in a classroom of your peers
ignoring the death sentence the world has; given less than twenty
years
try to understand the work it takes to break the simulation
because it's not just the Palestinians who are facing
extermination
soon you'll walk the stage at graduation in a fireproof suit and an
oxygen tank that they charged you for as part of your tuition

- degrees > celsius

i miss routine
and all the American things i can do

but when you've seen
all the American things we have done

the Coca-Cola bubbles, flatline
a bag of McDonald's becomes the bag that a little boy uses to
save what remains of his brothers flesh who was just blown to
pieces by an airstrike
the shampoos we use were made at the expense of an entire
neighborhood, desolated
the coffee, well, it's shit (Starbucks)
and if you like Amazon's free shipping
you'll love a FREE Palestine

i miss routine
but not enough to support a 6enocide.

supporting brands that fund the 6enocide of Gaza
makes you complicit...BOYCOTT!

use the Boycat app, or NoThanks! app to scan items at the store that
are directly tied to funding "Israel's" economy and their means to
afford weapons to kill children, and stop giving your money to those
companies. boycotting works! just look at what boycotting Disney
did when they removed the late night show host Jimmy Kimmel.
Disney lost BILLIONS overnight so they were forced to give Jimmy
his job back. hmm i wonder why "liberals" will boycott Disney when
a rich white man loses his job, but have no desire to boycott Disney
knowing Disney funds the slaughter of children in Gaza?

19

imagine viewing yourself as mentally weak
because you can't single handedly
stop the 6enocide in Gaza
but look at the world around you
take a look and you will see
people drinking Starbucks knowing that company
supports the slaughter of children
notice how no one is disrupting the status quo
those people are mentally weak
not you.

- "i'll take a venti gluttony please!"

*~~Google~~ BLACKROCK and its CEO Larry Fink

if words could save
maybe i'm not cut out to be the voice. the poet. the writer. the
author. the artist. the painter of words. the billboard for peace.

maybe 2Pac was wrong
and i won't "spark the brain that will change the world"

but those words will live on inside me for as long as i breathe.
inside the parts that cry and laugh and rage and pray and exist so
that i will never starve myself from the truth.
and to know, nothing, not even the dead silence of my
community will get me to join them.

maybe what wins in the end is humanity more entertained by
conspiracies and celebrity culture that eventually it's the only
thing that's real anymore.

and what i've written will have already been removed from these
digital shelves
and my existence, with it.

- Y2K let us down

here on earth
the right to breathe is on the chopping block
soon we'll be packaged and fed to cosmic voids
deprived of extravehicular mobility units
or simply put, spacesuits
and every form of currency will take our place
as prisoners of gravity
but more so, prisoners, of the ruling class

- AIPAC would fund a department of mass body disposals in NASA if they had
one (AIPAC is the American Israel Public Affairs Committee and they are most
likely responsible for the assassination of JFK).

in the year 2024
the Zionists control the American government

outlawing free speech
protected by the uprise of militant police and neo-nazis

and what's worse, the citizens are completely wiped of any
semblance of compassion. it must be international donut day or
get a free Starbucks for paying your portion of a 6enocide

there is little hope left to save a crumbling "democracy" and to
put an end to the ceaseless slaughter of innocent people

but the resistance remains steadfast
boycott! resist! and free Palestine!

- dystopia

by nature
we are selfish

by manufacturing
we are brainwashed

by choice
we are silent

and that in itself
is the problem

somewhere in the middle of
drawing a bath for your child
and readying supper for multiple mouths

there are children bathing
in their own gore, and being starved
for being born in an occupied town

- yet you're the one complaining
  about how hard your life is

imagine…
preaching about GOD in your music, on your instagram, to your
kids, on your podcast, at church, but never saying a single word
about the slaughter of over 20,000 children being broadcast live
everyday for the last 23 months and counting.

"If you've ever wondered what you would've done
during the **Holocaust**, you're doing it right now."
-unknown

the history of the world
is not all mystery
there are documented
wars and 6enocides
some of which we say
i love that era
the books and films that
portray these atrocities
i cannot believe people
suffered through those
dark times
#neveragain
so tell me,
are you waiting for the book
or the movie
to come out before you can
speak up about the side of
history your silence
tells me you're on?

- we all love a good holocaust movie to make us feel better about
ourselves BUT we all hate being bombarded with videos of
Palestinians being 6enocided by "Israel" in real time…if it's happening
in real life it's not worth our viewership…we like our feasts imaginary
so we can ask our friends if we look fat in this shirt, expecting them to
say no

in this era of mindless scrolling

where empathy goes to die

overstimulated by things that make you laugh

under-stimulated by things that make you cry

it's like watching a horror film

then going home to binge two seasons of Friends

the one where Phoebe runs

but not as fast as Palestinians run from 6enocide

- Ross Geller is a Zionist irl btw

twenty-five years into the millennium
the ship has been steered by wealthy men
time is being sold for starving wages
drinking water comes in plastic bottles
price-gouging is mistaken as inflation
housing is being used for vacations
pretty soon we'll rent the oxygen
and landlords will rewrite the Bible
and Muslims will be wiped from history
February will be too woke for southern states
so instead of adding one more day
they'll take away an entire month
and you won't say a word
or lift a finger for human rights
the children are f*cked

- what we allow them to get away with in Gaza will eventually make its way to the states. Gaza is the litmus test and we're FAILING as a collective world. but don't give up…that's exactly what they want us to do.

P.S. i wish Zionism was a conspiracy

maybe THIS 6enocide will be Christopher Nolan directed one
day?
maybe then the Oscars will have something to say?
maybe Leonardo DiCaprio will play 6enocide Joe once he's old
and gray?
except we all know Nolan has a thing for Inception so the truth
isn't always on display in plain sight
maybe it's day and night the way he directs vs. the journalists
who are actually losing their lives on camera?
maybe the material just isn't ripe for his taste?
maybe it's too early to say anything?
maybe the people he's inspiring are being wiped away?
maybe the science is still too hard to explain?
or maybe the bomb isn't big enough for the Americans'
privileged little brains?

- Oppenairprisonheimer

1.

this does not happen overnight
the occupation that they fight with rocks, paper, scissors against
bombs, tanks, and indoctrination
a breed too advanced in hate to save
one not dissimilar to third reich
the camps these days are American made
not gas, but paid for by you and i
how did we get here with advanced maps, hyper-connectivity,
and democracy?
they say history repeats itself, but it's not history
it's the people we entrust or don't trust whose power was passed
down to the people preaching peace with a gun to your head. the
people telling you I love you and God bless ONLY America.
they know the power of words. they know you'll stay silent
because they've been speaking for you
your entire life.
now you believe in capitalism more than human rights
now you believe racing to work is more stressful than running
from the new third Reich.

2.

"Israel's" society was built on the ethnic cleansing of
Palestinians from their homeland, Palestine, since 1948. if it's
mandatory as a citizen to join the "Israel" "Defense" Forces out
of high school, doesn't that make everyone in "Israel" guilty by
default? if you've served in the IDF, then you've witnessed and
participated in the crimes against innocent Palestinian children,
women, men, elderly, disabled, etc. this is the reason no "Israeli"
is innocent. and when they claim that Palestinians are raised to
kill and hate Jewish people, it's because the society called
"Israel" takes, steals, controls, imprisons, detains, blockades,

starves, carpet bombs, rapes, and plays psychological games with ALL of Palestine. this is not freedom, it's torture. it's apartheid. and it's been very much alive since the Nakba of 1948. (every accusation is a confession)

3.
to **erase** Palestine
is to get rich
both for "Israel" and the U.S.
and for all the neighboring Arab countries that are participating in the 6enocide of Gaza by remaining "**neutral**". just another way of saying "I stand with the oppressor". the greed is apparent but always clothed in propaganda and owning the narrative.
DOUBLE-SPEAK...
TRUMP: "I don't like what "ISRAEL" did."
ALSO TRUMP: "Here's more weapons. Just finish the job."

the only soulmate
barbaric in the fight
i may not send letters
but these words you
can hold tight
and if they ever sound
like cold weather
rest assured I wrote
them in delight
through gaslight and flame
the marauding of souls
the departing of lives
it was the ask of me
to find your light
and it showed
grayscale and stone
to be held without thorns
is to only accept a rose
as it's helpless and alone

- saving the world doesn't have to be lonely but it is

tired of small talk
tired of all talk no action
tired of justice for the rich
tired of Super Bowl ads for Zionists
tired of all of it not just some
tired of Amazon packages on every doorstep
tired of work but "i can't afford yet"
tired of laughing out loud with the ignorants
tired of forgetting i didn't really have parents
tired of suits that walk with confidence
tired of them talking about averages
tired of Arabs being called savages
tired of USA labeling themselves "God's Country"
tired of saying nothing while the IOF go hunting
tired of laid back tunes but rap ain't saying nothing
tired of praying but i was taught it does a lot
tired of believing in a halt. a ceasefire. a crooked cop
tired of Disney funding a 6enocide
tired of their subliminal messages for kids
tired of politics being left up to politicians
tired of politicians acting more like kids than kids
tired of Drake turning a blind eye like Taylor Swift

EVERYTHING CELEBRITY is a distraction from REALITY

all screens in technicolor
we post things for the world to discover
but when life brings you children and mothers your first reaction
is, is this real? the numbers?
since when did kills on the innocent become rewards? coffee and
burgers with M's and Stars free of charge?
i get that we're barely making it as it is
and the small town that you live is too expensive to raise a kid
too busy hanging on by a thread that you read from some news
source you depend
with shallow coverage of children, men, and women all dropped
off at the deep end. weights tied to their legs
we waste time in L.A. trying to *Save Mr. Banks*
instead of saving for a rainy day, we watch the rain pour
on top of tents and displaced babies
but nothing compares to the carpet bombs on hospitals filled
with patients outpacing the amount of doctors also waiting to be
seen
meanwhile the scenes don't get less nauseating
i hear the grass is green on the other side where God is waiting
and the hands are red on the government you and i are
fundraising

meet me by the orchard
the last place they shall bomb
maybe they'll change their mind, not bury missiles in our front lawn
to tell the truth I'm terrified for all the eyes that watch as our deaths become normalized
my neighbor was a poet. his father was a teacher. his wife was a doctor. but their lives are no longer. so it's just you and i and his daughter. we're not surprised she doesn't cry, she's from the same earth where there's no time to grieve our neighbors. we are not soldiers, we're martyrs of our land. they wield your weapons in their hands with no discretion for whom they're aimed at. a mother with a broom. a little brother folding his prayer mat. we're no different than you. except you're in a cozy room watching your daughter as she naps. you know a bag of chips would wake her and so would the sound of bombs you watch on Instagram aimed at children younger than the one you hatched.

- cover your ears darling, you're gonna wanna see this

if social media didn't exist
and i saw you in person
our conversation would be about work. marriage.
weather. and kids.
and whatever the newspaper hid we would never know
especially if our group of friends have the same color skin and
Arab countries have been categorized as terrorists by the
government
and the church goers are far from angelic
our conversation would not be about the new nazis
small talk would just be small talk
just like it is now
as we all watch the bombs drop like everyday
is New Year's Eve
another mother, father, and child, gone.

wanting to see the world but not its problems
while ignoring the ones in your own town
(a good ol' American pastime)

i'm trying to define the universe
knowing there's more impurities here on earth
wondering where smiles come from these days because
i try to crack a smile and it hurts
knowing there's a child whose worth is less than
wholesale value of your designer purse
less than your "hard work" and even worse, their life is less than
words you serve the public
and public figures love to preach that whatever you put out into
the universe, you receive tenfold
then watch as tents housing the displaced get bulldozed
i'm trying to define the universe and find my role here on earth
they're not just souls they're God's gift worth more than gold or
any sifting and digging you can do to mine the loaves of bread
we call bountiful
bountiful to whom?
you have more than enough but enough is never enough
so you sell their souls too
money can buy a 6enocide but it can't buy forgiveness
since you claim you're religious too

- "hypocrisy hotline. this is your politician speaking"

the stations of the cross
is a reminder that someone
had to document the truth about Jesus' suffering
because his oppressors made him look like
the t e r r o r i s t
much like our media is doing today
against innocent Palestinians who
are from the birthplace of Jesus Christ
P A L E S T I N E

- God's country is not the U.S. sorry to break it to ya

P.S. even the journalists who documented the murder of Jesus weren't killed
like how Israel kills journalists to hide their crimes. **over 270 journalists
murdered by "Israel"** so far (not including the journalists they're killing in other
Arab countries as we speak)

what is normal?
we tell ourselves that our
simple everyday pleasures
and luxuries are normal
but that our shortcomings
are attacks on our sanity
a tax, some say, on humanity
your car breaks down
your pants no longer fit
your friends outgrew you
it rains a little bit and
you throw a fit asking why
god would do this to you
all of it, your whining
exists at the same time over
a hundred children lose their
lives, daily. and to them this
has become normal. not knowing
why they are running, but run
with no time to worry about
bathing or the disappearing sun
because every day feels like night
as we fill our darkness with
Christmas trees and gifted guns
we call this normal where we're from.

psychosis is defined as a break from reality
but a break from reality would mean more lives turn into
casualties
i know it's not the same thing because in psychosis we
experience what isn't real
but on Thanksgiving we pretend there's not a 6enocide
happening while we enjoy our meals
i'm guilty just as well
but it would be a crime to have a voice and not use it
to have a platform and act stupid like we don't see all people as
human
because those children, men, and women have a name and a
conscience. they could be outside playing in the garden instead
of laying under cement. they could use a break from reality, just
like some of us do on Thanksgiving. they too have love to give,
and bellies to feed. they too have centuries of a homeland. *from
the river to the sea*. from this little break from reality your table
should be filled with love for EVERYONE, not just a full plate
of turkey. for the love of all people, especially the ones that are
still missing
…under the rubble

- psychosis (written Thanksgiving 2023)

i think warm thoughts during winter
i think about mom and dad over dinner
the thing about plans is they never turn out the way we hoped we
would remember
i planned to be done writing a book by December (2023)
but i never planned to watch more than 60,000 people get
slaughtered, and the survivors still manage to put God first.
cause when he took my parents from me
he was the first i chose to desert
the first to know i was hurt
and the last person i thought would emerge from the cries
we ask how any of this is justified?
march, post, protest in different parts of the earth. more lies to
demoralize but can never break their spirit or worth. and from
their courage i learn just how privileged i am to have the luxury
of concern about my **mental health**. how could anyone believe
so strongly these people deserve to pull bodies from the rubble?
homes to be leveled and babies shoveled? while we think warm
thoughts in the safety of our un-bombed homes and little
bubbles.

- privilege is: prioritizing mental health to ignore a 6enocide

i still have my morning coffee from home.
laughter that reaches my bones and cures whatever i'm going
through. i have the remaining breath of my ancestors, oxygen
that isn't free to all of us. i want to say that i'm not busy looking
down at my phone or looking up at it as i thank god i'm awake.
and you may not get that text back from me. i hope you don't
wait up, because you know that's me. and you know that if I'M
posting it's because there are issues larger than ours but i'll still
complain about slammed doors, ignored chores, sports bars that
celebrate while a 6enocide wages on the innocent. and i'm the
one serving unlimited amounts of spirits. meanwhile, more
spirits are being sent to the same place you pray your loved ones
went.
the difference is you had no say in their mortalities like you do
with the people wishing they could be doing nothing but live a
life with human rights and dignity.

- no time to mourn in Gaza

before Christmas
we give weapons to the occupation forces
and now that it's almost Thanksgiving
we will feed and shelter the homeless for a day
bless the table, burn the turkey, and watch the Macy's parade
we'll say thanks be to God on Sundays
but where have these prayers gone?
were they sent to president orange or potus bob?
to let old Saint Nick deliver gifts of mass destruction to kill our
kids, women, and husbands, the innocent?
i say OUR because the hours are the same no matter which time
zone you're in
their time is just as precious, if not more precious than yours,
mine, and his

- written before Xmas of 2023

for the last 8 months (August 20, 2025) Gaza has been starved and deprived of all aid from entering its borders (by the "Israeli" Occupation Forces). so the U.S. and "Israel's" solution is to take over the UN's job distributing aid. they hire private U.S. military contractors to act as a third party impartial distributor. they call themselves the Gaza Humanitarian Foundation, or, GHF for short. but we call them the Gaza Humiliation Death Traps because that's exactly what they are, DEATH TRAPS. they lure in starving Palestinians (because "Israel" is starving them) and kill them. they found a way that seems less like a crime than gas chambers in Auschwitz, that their ancestors were placed in during the holocaust. they found a way to murder starving Palestinians that doesn't look as criminal. and because they own western media, and don't let any journalists into Gaza to document these crimes, while also holding the record for most journalists (Palestinian) killed in a "war zone" over 270, people around the world are normalizing these crimes and honestly they don't care that it's happening. these crimes can be seen on the screen of your phone. there's no excuse.

this modern day holocaust is being ignored when we are living in a time where information is the easiest to access. knowing there's a 6enocide, and saying nothing, should feel like a crime on your moral conscience. there's no excuse!

i don't know where to start
but i'll tell you that while thousands are being starved to death
and killed in Gaza, i have friends who are inviting me out.
they've seen my posts about donating to families in Gaza who
are starving or have lost multiple if not hundreds of family
members to "Israeli" attacks and U.S. bombs. they've seen me
ask for help, but they never help. yet, they have the audacity to
ask me if i want to go out and drink or have dinner. how could i
justify spending over $75 stuffing my face at a restaurant and
drinking till i pass out, knowing that money could go to a family
that needs to survive forced starvation and displacement? Gazans
have to survive the destruction of their homes, their
neighborhoods, their schools, their markets, their hospitals, their
families, their people, and their land.
i will admit, i've had my moments of weakness.
but there's nothing to celebrate about.
you might say a birthday or Christmas are good reasons. but if
you took just a second to not be selfish, newborns are being
killed in Gaza daily. and because most of the world is incapable
of having empathy for the all out extermination of Palestinians,
then no, i have no empathy for the lack of Christmas presents
under your tree, or lack of birthday wishes from me.
let me know when you wish me a free Palestine. and instead of
requesting gifts on any holiday, ask your friends to please donate
to Gaza.

you don't report back to
most messages on your phone
partly because you're overwhelmed
partly because you're depressed
partly because of spam messages
partly because you don't have the answers
partly because you don't want to hurt anyone's feelings

but ALL because you'd rather spend your time writing as a form
of resistance
you'd rather show up with something to give, than to be empty
handed
so wait on it
i know i'm the bad guy for not responding to your messages
but you would understand if you knew these words are for the
martyrs and for the living who are trying to survive weapon
testing and nonstop bombs raining down on their bodies, wiping
entire families and lineages off the face of the earth. bombs
cratering sandy areas filled with displaced families in their
makeshift tents, evaporating bodies but they still dig.

- radicalize yourself like i did and stop being an itch-bay

i wonder if Jesus "the carpenter" built furniture for royalty?

my best friend's roommate spends hours on their day off learning how to fix the washer and dryer in their laundry room. we got back to their place at night and it seemed they were able to fix whatever the issue was. i know they felt proud, and rightfully so they shoulda been. but after all that hard work, and because they were too "tired" to cook the endless amount of food rotting in their refrigerator, they were rewarded with a giant bag of McDonald's catered by their partner. somehow, after previously informing them McDonald's is being boycotted because they feed the Nazi army of "Israel" in between killing children in Gaza with U.S. made weapons. maybe it was something i said because they took my comment seriously by going out of their way to support a company that is explicitly feeding an army that slaughters children and their families.
i will remember this blatant disregard for humanity that my friends roommate and their partner thinks is a joke, with all their fucking privilege in their safe little bubbles of nothing like the rest of us, living paycheck to paycheck for decades without question. maybe if our country stopped sending billions of dollars to "Israel" to kill thousands of innocent people, none of us would be so poor and morally bankrupt?
just, maybe.

*this pertains to everyone i know still silent and taking zero action. so if you're feeling some type of way, that's the point. 99% of my friends and family give zero attention to the 6enocide in Gaza (McDonald's is franchise owned, i know, but it's principle)

i just learned of your name, Madea
the lady in all pink
i just learned of your name because the empire is good at
suppressing radical voices for peace, justice, and liberation.
and because we're only supposed to know the names of
deceased political activists, because to know of any who
are still alive and are still fighting against the prejudices of
the world and our country, would be detrimental to the
propaganda machine of the empire controlled media.
you speak like you've read a book or two, but more
importantly you speak from the heart and for the people.
and when I see you confront our politicians who are
sending the bombs to kill Palestinian men, women, and
children their reactions are telling...
they are immediately filled with rage and their tempers
surge from having to suppress the truth.
you ask them if the children of Gaza cry differently than
children anywhere else? and they respond by calling you a
terrorist, and that you receive money from Iran, Qatar, and
China (their way of saying, "I'm racist")
these are the people we let govern our country and that we
call "leaders"
but they've been put in these positions strategically by the
American Israel Public Affairs Committee (AIPAC) for
decades
they say racist remarks effortlessly and naturally, and that's
partly because they've realized that the majority of the

public have shown they don't care enough and there are no crimes big enough to make them care. so these so-called leaders say whatever they want including Islamophobic slurs, but their actions are a lot worse than their words.
i am learning through your courageous actions,
Madea Benjamin
may the rest of the world take a page from your playbook because i am sick and tired, as i'm sure you are, of watching babies in Gaza starve to their last breaths, and take bullets to an under developed heart and between the eyes by trained elite snipers from the Israeli Occupation Forces.

- CODEPINK

The Different Levels of Empathy for Gaza
(which one are you?)

Extreme empathy: self-immolation (lighting oneself on fire in protest)
Very Bold empathy: hunger strike (not eating/fasting as a form of protest). joining a freedom flotilla (boats to break the siege on Gaza)
Mindful empathy: changing your lifestyle to reflect the suffering or depravity that Gaza is facing in order to feel their pain in some small way (for instance, be mindful of consumption, fast daily, and boycott EVERYTHING...get creative)
Moderate empathy: boycotts damn near everything that contributes to the 6enocide of Gaza, joins protests, but also still likes being social and goes to parties or clubs to feel less alone
Meh! empathy: boycotts some businesses but doesn't prioritize Gaza as the highest of importance and would rather sulk in their own misery until someone feels sorry for them, and when no one feels sorry for them they call the movement of people standing up for Gaza, fake friends, for not being there for them when in reality watching children get killed everyday for 704 days takes its toll and it becomes hard to be there for the friends in our own circles because no one is there for us, obviously (but for real it's hard to be there for friends when millions of people in Gaza need us to be their voice and be strong for them)
Eh! empathy: "awww it's so sad what's happening" (never hear from them again, but post their food, vacations, material shit on social media, but can't afford to donate to the forcibly starved and forcibly displaced before they're murdered by the IOF)

one side wields all the power

"they cut the electricity
and light the sky with missiles"

who would dare pick up the camera?
put on the vest?

expose. shoot. expose.

why are they killing journalists?

i'm asking

YOU

the READER

why?

supPRESSion for propaganda

/intifada/ in-tea-fah-the *(thanks Dina for correcting me :)*

U.S. politicians and mainstream media love to spin the word "intifada" as a word meaning "terrorist". but just so you know, intifada is an Arabic word meaning, "uprising".
would there need to be an uprising if Palestine was free from its colonizer? if their colonizer wasn't stealing their land everyday for 77 years? if their colonizers weren't killing their children and their people with impunity from white supremacy western civilization for 77 years? did October 7th happen as a result of all the crimes Palestinians have to endure because "Jewish" people can only be "safe" if they steal and 6enocide Palestine? does Gaza, Palestine not have the right to defend itself from the illegal tyranny of "Israel"? is forcibly starving an entire population of 2 million people (50% children) "defense"? is dropping 8 times the amount of Hiroshima bombs on one of the most densely populated lands while keeping them caged in considered "defense"? if you change the name, Gaza, to New York City, would New York City have the right to defend itself?

for my Americans reading this...why the f*ck do U.S. politicians have to "voluntarily" visit "Israel" when they're elected? what kind of culty bullshit is that? are we a Jewish or Chrisitian country? NO! but we are a Zionist owned country. Zionists were declared a "form of racism and racial discrimination" in 1975 by the United Nations General Assembly because they colonized the INDIGENOUS people of Palestine. you're telling me you wouldn't UPRISE??

if you care at all about Gaza or humanity, create an Instagram account and follow these Palestinian voices/accounts, and visit the links in their bios to save lives. this is Gaza's main source of reaching the outside world:

@wizard_bisan1
@motaz_azaiza
@mosab_abutoha
@middleeasteye
@eye.on.palestine
@alaydi2023
@wearthepeace
@humantiproject
@gazafreedomflotilla
@jenanmatari
@hossam_shbat
@renadfromgaza
@leenfromgaza
@anasjamal44
@thesameerproject
@operationolivebranch
@salem_alaydi_
@monterey_palestine_solidarity
@ebaa.gaza
@celebrities4palestine
@mariambarghouti
@codepinkalert
@letstalkpalestine (join broadcast channel)
@palestine_protect
@amna_alaydi

"Israel" receives so much free money to invest in the exploitation of technology for surveillance and advanced weapons because they've convinced the world that Palestinians are "animals" who need to be surveilled (and most of that money comes from American taxpayers).

you don't become one of the wealthiest "nations" in the world (with little debt) without the backing of THE wealthiest nation in the world (with trillions in debt) who spends ten times the amount on military, and weapons manufacturing than the top 5 largest militaries in the world COMBINED; including China and Russia.

think about it, the U.S. doesn't really do anything to deserve to be the wealthiest nation, they just fearmonger the rest of the world into submission for their resources, while keeping the "working class" always on the verge of homelessness. the U.S. are thieves who extract with greed and the MIGHT of their military. this is what an empire does, they conquer! they do not conform with International Law, nor do they help other countries in the best interest of the countries they claim to be "helping". meanwhile, American citizens are too busy to realize this because they're the ones trying to get rich off of those stolen resources from MINERAL RICH countries that we label POOR.

- fact check me please (and if i'm wrong, being closely accurate to these numbers should still push you to take action) there are people who will tell you

"i can't look at what's happening in Gaza because it's too sad
and depressing"

these are the same people doing absolutely nothing to stop the
6enocide

if you're not strong enough to bear witness
the bare minimum you can do is be their voice

and not support brands that fund the killing

- Boycott. Divest. Sanction (BDS) website : bdsmovement.net

Apps to download:
Boycat
Disoccupied
NoThanks!

it's not always the algorithm that hides the crimes
it's also the people who see you posting everyday for
689 days the dead bodies of children, the cries for help,
the forced starvation
these so-called friends on social media are purposely ignoring
your posts
they are sick and tired of feeling guilty for not caring about the
mass slaughter of human beings

remember that it doesn't concern them because it's not
happening in America or to their family
it's just happening because of America and because of THEIR
silence.

- true colors

they shoot at the limbs of children, and private parts
of teenage boys
to immobilize them, and to cause suffering to their future
making them amputees and killing their chances of reproduction
and to be an amputee in a "war zone" means you cannot run
from the daily bombs
you cannot carry aid back to your tent where your entire family
was just murdered
and in some cases amputees in Gaza, out of thousands, are
having their limbs sawn off with household objects and no
anesthesia
and the pain of losing a limb, need i say it?
KILLS

- Palestinian children are the largest group of child amputees in modern
history (because of "Israel") … just ask Ms. Rachel

the amount of bombs "Israel" has dropped on Gaza has surpassed the
equivalent of

6

Hiroshima

bombs

for the visual learners out there
and i think they've surpassed **8** Hiroshimas by now
September 9, 2025

Quotes

"Our information ecology is poisoned."
- Naomi Klein

"They dehumanize you to get away with brutalizing you."
- Zein Rahma

"If i must die, you must live to tell my story…"
- Refaat Alareer (poem)

"The U.S. is divided into two classes: the servant class, and those we serve."
- @iamblakeley (instagram)

"We're not freeing Palestine. Palestine is freeing us."
- unknown (but remember it)

"You can kill a revolutionary, but you can't kill the revolution."
- Fred Hampton (leader of the Illinois chapter of the Black Panther Party)

"Being alive is weird…so we gotta embrace each other."
- Steve Lacy

"The hands that help are holier than the lips that pray."
- unknown

"Gaza became the cemetery for international law and humanity."
- Rula Jebreal

"I see God himself in the eye of a refugee."
- Anees (Hinds Hall 2)

"

Were there not an Israel, the United States would have to invent an Israel to protect her interests in the region.

- 6enocide Joe (Biden)

what exactly are the United States' interests in the region?

it starts with POLITICIANS

they set the precedent for war
they create the salaries to entice teenagers to join the armed
forces

they use majority of tax dollars on military spending and
weapons manufacturing

they prioritize military first because politicians make their largest
personal PROFIT off of war (inside trading)

they retire or lose their positions in government, then join a
lobby group for a giant corporation (the political term for bribing
politicians is called lobbying. and it's LEGAL. but you will not
outbid a corporation's "donation" to get your policy seen. you
have to fight back in a REAL democratic way which takes longer
than just throwing money at people in power who claim to be
working for the people)

the cycle of corruption in our government is why we don't have
"public servants" in this "democracy", we have POLITICIANS
and WARMONGERS and SELF-SERVERS
and OLIGARCHY

- they are no one special. they're human like you and me. stop treating them like they're
invincible or some sort of god who's gonna save you. most of them were born rich or sell
you a story about their "rough" childhood. red and blue don't care about you…it's profit
over people at the end of the day for them. "CONGRESS LOVES ENDLESS WAR."
-Medhi Hasan

some people are out having
cosmic feelings and revelations

and to them this is the secret to life and fulfillment

this is a fairytale way of thinking
and the world needs that sometimes
but not while Gaza is being 6enocided by
"Israel" and the U.S.

FUCK your fairytale.

you're gonna end up heartbroken and wanting sympathy
and when you finally snap out of it, a million Palestinians will
have already been murdered by "Israel"

if the people of Gaza are being deprived of cosmic feelings and
revelations
then we all need to put ours on hold

fairytales are made when everyone is free, not just some

- fairytales are for the FREE (and none of us are free until we're
all free)

P.S. **Disney** funds the 6enocide in Gaza. how's that for a fairytale?

P.P.S. we all deserve to find love in this world. i hope you find it. but you
should know **Dr. Rolla Alaydi** has lost over 200 loved ones since October 2023
to 6enocide by "Israel". if you're looking for love, make sure that person
doesn't support 6enocide.

under the rubble
you'll find stories
of people who lived magnificent lives you might call
ordinary
and it's this illusion we hold that things that are ordinary,
don't hold magic
those stories that lie there, under the rubble, were
dehumanized to your liking
as long as they were labeled "animals", they had no right to
exist
and because you don't value your ordinary life, you
devalue the ordinary of others

under the rubble
you'll find entire families
children who took cover under their mothers arms
or some that were in separate rooms playing dolls, while
mom and dad prepared a family meal
fresh bread
the everpresent smell of spices
and olive oil
all of it
homes, toys, televisions, family rooms, reduced to powder
and pieces

under the rubble
newly weds and wrapping paper
till death do us part
vowed and sealed

under the rubble
screams for help become prayer for life, become the arms
reach for air, become not the heart's failure to pump blood,
but the calling home of, the innocent

- inspired by **Mosab Abu Toha**

picture your local news team
imagine them, their camera crew, and their entire
on the ground journalists were all killed
every single one of them
murdered by airstrikes

but the way mainstream media coverage reported
their deaths was in two words, **"found" "dead"**
not who killed them or how (it's no secret)
because to know where the news team was from
is to assume they deserved it
to assume that the people who killed them
are never wrong and had the right to "defend"
themselves against **journalists**

and to share the real reason they were killed
would likely cost mainstream media "journalists"
their job or future
but to report anything BUT the truth
is grounds for satire news, not real journalism
and should be illegal to be called "newsworthy"

- if you expose "Israel's" **crimes**, you're ANTISEMITIC

"Israel" has **killed** over **270** journalists in **Gaza** including every last **Al Jazeera** journalist. this is the highest number of journalists killed in all recent wars combined, and that's because it's not a war, it's a 6enocide.

the bees have fled the land

uneased by artificial buzzing of drones orbiting children at play,
for 24-hours, outlasting the sun

drones that use modern day technology
updating on the fly
lurking amongst the rubble
surveilling
bidding on facial recognition
whether controlled by a soldier remotely operated
or fully autonomous, making decisions at the behest
of some tech-bros flawless coding embedded into
the drones natural born DNA of spotting "terrorists"
if only these drones knew who the real
terrorists are…

- even the bees are at risk of being "collateral damage"

      when Palestinians see the birds or the bees still playing amongst the
      rubble, a tiny bit of hope is restored. but for how long before the
      bombs fall again? here they come…

people still ask

do you remember what you were doing when NINE ELEVEN happened?

BRO!
where were you when the U.S. sent billions of dollars in bombs and aid to "Israel" to commit a 6enocide against Gaza for 2 years while it was being livestreamed on your phone???

- by the way **the U.S. murdered over a million people** in Iraq, Afghanistan, and all over the Arab region, killing mostly women and children. the **9/11** lie gave the U.S. an excuse to begin the so-called "WAR ON TERROR"…and i was rollerskating at 5am Pacific Standard Time if you really must know

P.S. there's a lot of accurate accounts and speculation that "Israel" was behind the 9/11 terrorist attacks. do with that information what you will.

what will you be remembered by?
what will you be remembered by?
what will you be remembered by?
what will you be remembered by?
what will you be remembered by?
what will you be remembered by?
what will you be remembered by?
what will you be remembered by?
what will you be remembered by?
what will you be remembered by?
what will you be remembered by?
what will you be remembered by?
what will you be remembered by?
when you know there's a 6enocide!!
what will you be remembered by?
what will you be remembered by?
what will you be remembered by?
what will you be remembered by?
what will you be remembered by?j
what will you be remembered by?
what will you be remembered by?
what will you be remembered by?
what will you be remembered by?
what will you be remembered by?
what will you be remembered by?
what will you be remembered by?
what will you be remembered by?
what will you be remembered by?
what will you be remembered by?

your silence

have you ever prayed for the devil?
so why would you start now?

-    praying for "Israel"

if i could convince you to do anything
it wouldn't be to donate to families in Gaza (that should come
from the heart and being selfless…)
it would be to radicalize yourself against the propaganda
of the oppressor
they all want to be your friend
they're friendly people as long as you don't reveal their crimes
or their wrongdoings (local law enforcement)
but beware
have you ever put unquestionable trust in someone you thought
you knew inside out?
have you ever tried to confront that person for doing something
you didn't agree with?
what was their reaction?
did they show a hostile side of themselves that you never would
have imagined they had in them?
if someone you love is great at keeping secrets, but even more
emotionally destructive when those secrets are revealed, what do
you think a powerful and corrupt government and military are
capable of when you expose them for what they've always been?

- gaslighting in the middle of global warming and 6enocide…nobody light a
match

for all you *Avatar The Last Airbender* fans out there aka me

choose one

<u>the fire nation</u>   <u>the Avatar</u>
"Israel"   Palestine

YIP
YIP

the fire lord wants us to believe there can be only one Avatar
there are 8 billion of us, there can be 8 billion Avatars
Save Gaza

there's this excuse we make when the troubles of the world seem
not to directly affect us where we live

it's called "not my problem"

and for some of us it's called, being racist
ignorant, or Islamophobic
mainstream media is an expert at portraying
damn near all Arab people as TERRORISTS
or the bad guy
and we fall for it every time.

- if the 6enocide was happening to a white European country, you wouldn't be
able to shut up about it…the war in Ukraine is a war but some people see it as a
6enocide the longer it progresses. but just look how much attention it gets from
the media without PASSIVE VOICE. Ukraine has a formal military and
receives weapons and aid from the U.S., Gaza doesn't have a military. Hamas is
a group of guys retaliating and fighting for freedom from their illegal occupier
and the people who control their every move and breath.

- there are Jewish, and Christian, and Catholic Arabs too. not all Arabs are
Muslim (not all Jews are white). but even if they were all Muslim, Muslim
people are kind, full of love, the keepers of the key, and very generous. we have
to be mindful of our upbringings, that many of us have been sheltered and have
never had Muslim or Arab friends. if that's the case we need to stop making
judgements about some stereotype or assumption that Arab and Muslim people
are terrorists. it would be similar to calling ALL white people KKK or Nazis
(sidenote: the KKK still exists and President Trump thinks they're nice people).
politicians are always fostering bad blood between us to keep us divided while
they team up with billionaires who profit from us hating each other. billionaire
and millionaire politicians create conflict between two societies to distract us
from the corrupt things they're doing in the background.

for the millennial parents reading this…

remember in the 1990's when our parents would tell us to finish our food because children in other countries are starving?

c'mon i know i'm not the only one (or maybe its a poor people thing?). but do you remember how you felt when your parents would say those words to you?

i mean, i still struggled to finish my food, but that little "lie" got me to eat what i could.

and i suspect parents still use that little lie to this day.

fast forward to the present day, watching the 6enocide and forced starvation of Palestinian children, mothers, fathers, and the entire population of Gaza. have you sat your kids down to tell them that "Israel" is murdering and starving children in Gaza? that might be a good reason for them to appreciate having food so easily available.

how is it that we shelter our children from the brutal reality that other children are living? is it because we've been indoctrinated into keeping secrets for the "greater good"?

or is it the fear of not knowing enough to weigh in on the **6enocide** against Palestinian children?

are you raising your child to befriend ALL children including Palestinian children? i believe children have the innate sense of love for all people and they would share their food and be courteous to the children suffering in Gaza in a heartbeat…as would children in Gaza do the same for your kids. we could learn a thing or two about empathy from children.

if we keep sheltering the children in our nation from seeing the reality of the rest of the world, or even the reality in some of our communities, kids will likely have to unlearn a lot, like us millennials are doing right now.

- TG for Ms. Rachel for littles, and Mr. Rogers lol

pro-Palestine is pro-humanity
and so is…

anti-Zionist
anti-6enocide
anti-ethnostate
anti-capitalism
anti-christian nationalist
anti-settler colonialism
anti-white supremacy
anti-holocaust
anti-AIPAC
anti-fascist
anti-war
anti-oligarchy
anti-forced starvation
anti-collateral damage
anti-ethnic cleansing
anti-illegal occupation
airstrike —>   anti-authoritarianism
anti-apartheid
anti-nazi
anti
ant
a

baby —>   .

THESE PEOPLES LIVES ARE BEING BROADCAST EVERYDAY BLOODIED, IN PIECES, MANGLED, HEAVING, HOLDING ONTO LIFE THAT DOESN'T SEEM WORTH HOLDING ONTO. LIVESTREAMED ARE THE MOST TRAGIC SCENES THEY'LL EVER EXPERIENCE. THE MOST TRAGIC SCENES WE'LL EVER EXPERIENCE. YOU MIGHT FEEL HELPLESS THAT YOUR POSTS ON SOCIAL MEDIA AREN'T STOPPING THE 6ENOCIDE, BUT WHILE YOU FEEL HELPLESS, THEIR ORGANS AND THEIR HEADLESS BODIES ARE BEING EXPOSED TO THE WORLD, NORMALIZED IN BETWEEN EVERY MEME AND EVERY TEXT MESSAGE RINGING OFF YOUR PHONE.

724 DAYS OF ONGOING ANNIHILATION
we should all be sick to our stomachs and organizing against our politicians funding the genocide.

the resistance of the Palestinian people is the byproduct of colonization and the illegal occupation of their land and psyche for 77 years. there is no argument that can be made to justify the 6enocide. not only is "Israel" not a real place, but "Israel" also prides itself on being the most "moral army" as if there could ever be such a thing. "Israel" also claims to be the "holy land" created for the "chosen people" by God. and because they hold themselves to such high regard as the "chosen people", they actually believe they are superior beings. sound familiar, Nazis?? read that again. "Israels" society believes they are superior beings in comparison to the rest of the world. and just to clarify, shouldn't the most "moral army" and the "chosen people" by God, actually have "morals" rather than murder over a hundred Palestinians a day for over 700 days now? it's not defense when you're the one murdering mass amounts of people every f*cking day. the logic right?

but how could people have logic without having the correct information? logic is a byproduct of knowing the truth. and NO i don't mean the kind of "truth" President Trump and his cult followers arm themselves with. but we are living in a time when someone who has a massive following on social media is given an unchecked power of influence, and could easily spread false information to people who are susceptible to propaganda, as well as stubborn when proven wrong, or proven guilty.

when you've been calling it a 6enocide for the last 2 years, but the media still refrains from making the "assumption" that 20,000 murdered children is in fact a 6enocide, you start to go a little fucking crazy.

w o r d s   m a t t e r .

the more our world leaders and media call it a "war", the less accountability they'll face. and the longer we allow them to get away with downplaying the all out extermination of Gaza, the more crimes they'll get away with in our own countries. it won't just stop at Gaza. who's next?

this is the world some people wish to raise their kids in. leave them with the mess you made, right?

- the "stir crazy" of Covid is a cake walk compared to the stir crazy of watching a livestreamed 6enocide (especially when the 6enocide has far outlasted the Covid lockdown period...making this comparison absolutely disgusts me btw)

these people are real.
they frequent cafes
they celebrate weddings
they graduate universities
they become doctors
they raise children
they write poetry
they contribute globally
they breathe
have heartbeats
have memories
make music
make love
try to survive
try to provide for their families and neighbors
they sing beautiful melodies
in a beautiful language, older than ours
they telephone to say i love you
they pray into the sky
and worship the earth
and that is why
when the earth cracks
whether a smile or when it feels broken
they fall into it
the way seeds fall

- Palestine belongs to Palestinians (evolution means giving back to the soil of your ancestors)

1.

every prayer should come with action
if you're praying before every meal, is it to give thanks for the
food? or to say sorry for wasting it in advance when you know
people are being starved to death, and you're on your 5th meal of
the day...there is no shortage for you, but it's not something you
think about. why would you, right?

2.

i've become short tempered and easily agitated with the people i
love, because they've been more silent than my cold shoulder.
they want the best for their children, so they spoil them, never
teaching them there are children in Gaza who only wish for a
warm meal, their parents, and to go to school. and because some
of them secretly support the **sadistic** acts of the apartheid state of
"Israel" (fake ass Christians). Americans love to shelter their kids
from reality
and it's a disgrace to be honest.
but one thing i've noticed, if this younger generation ever
decides to take anything seriously, is that they are fed up
with the 6enocide in Gaza, and always feeling gaslit by
their elders (something the older generation has long been too
afraid, prideful, or silenced to ever speak up about). the younger
generation is "standing on business" screaming at the older
generation to stop being racist, xenophobic, homophobic,
Islamophobic, and just all around judgmentally-ill people...who
by the way preach being kind, but do the exact opposite behind
closed doors, unless emboldened by someone like Trump to say
the quiet part out loud and get away with it. just sayin.

we're not protesting, we're mourning.

have you seen the news?

maybe not on television, but it's all over social media.

maybe they can televise the 6enocide in between the weather and sports?

i wonder what that would sound like?

let's go to our weather man in "Israel" to tell us the weather in Gaza…

oh hey, Don!

expect thunder today. bombs will be raining down.

make sure you take your most sentimental belongings because you won't have a home to go back to.

oh, and pack lite. everything you own has to fit miraculously inside a single garbage bag. and i hope you packed your hiking boots, you're gonna need them for the mountains of rubble on the road to "safety".

where is safety you ask?

hold on, let me finish printing these leaflets that we'll drop on you, giving you 15 minutes to evacuate before we drop the next wave of U.S. made bombs…

here, go to the south where it's "safe".

THE SOUTH IS BEING MASSACRED

well, you can't stay here and you can't leave Gaza…

i guess you'll have to play our game and try to survive.

the catch is, you only get one life.

subtract three hearts from the top right portion of the screen.

much better.

GOOD LUCK! and stay dry.

it's forbidden to acknowledge the existence of Palestinians without being considered **antisemitic** by Zionist Jews and Zionist U.S. politicians. but let's take a look at the definition of the word, semite, according to the dictionary:

Semite
a member of any of the peoples who speak or spoke a Semitic language, including in particular the Jews and Arabs.

so by definition Arabs and Jews are Semites. now remember, before Zionists started their propaganda to steal the land of Palestine in 1948, Jewish people lived in harmony with Muslim, Christian, and Jewish Palestinians in Palestine. **Zionist Jews** do not practice traditional Jewish values (Judaism). and Jewish people cannot be categorized into a single race. most Zionist Jews are Ashkenazi Jews (a Jewish person of central or eastern European descent, traditionally speaking Yiddish; **NOT Hebrew**). The founder of Zionism, Theodor Herzl, was atheist.

- why do U.S. politicians cover for the Zionist state of "Israel" and their crimes? because many of those politicians are dual citizens of the U.S. and "Israel", some are Jewish, majority of them are Zionist and funded by AIPAC and other Jewish lobby groups, and many of them are Christian Nationalists who believe the U.S. should be run on Christian values, not democratic ones. also note: **Christian Nationalists**, and **Christian Zionists** are extremists with antisemitic tropes embedded within their belief system (and they don't hide it very well either)

if Palestinians didn't care about politics,
they'd just be wondering why bombs are
being dropped on them every day.
it's not because of terrorist militaries like
the U.S. and "Israel", or resistance groups like Hamas.
it's because of politicians. they have a lot to gain.
their politics are the reason soldiers kill each other.
and why civilians end up with a higher death toll.
HUMANITY is politics.
politicians get to decide whether we're allowed "human rights".
they determine whether we're worthy to be alive.
whether our lives, especially Palestinian lives are worth more
than their extravagant lifestyles.
and they make these decisions with our tax dollars.
and they get rich doing it, playing with our lives,
hate-mongering, and cashing in on it.
and the military is too young and dumb to think for themselves.
they don't join the armed forces to do good.
they join to escape whatever hell they're already
living in.

- besides the money, don't forget about their xenophobia

- keep in mind the people who vote for these politicians still fall for the lies of
the two party system in America. we still vote for the lesser of two evils, or the
party that makes the most unrealistic promises but never delivers because
duuuuh, greed!!! stop falling for the democratic lie. and if you believe anything
the republicans say, i'll pray for you.

what will it take for you to break your silence?
another child's body charred, dismembered, found in pieces
inside their makeshift tent poorly pitched in a "safe zone"?
another university detonated with high level explosives? another
recruit from America who wishes death upon Palestinian
children?
another politician who's stealing your money to kill kids, making
you believe those kids are "terrorists!"?
another hundred murdered in a day, because that's everyday
since October 7th?

we're starting to see the people who have been silent about the
6enocide are now grossed out by the forced starvation "Israel" is
engineering on an entire population of around 2 million people in
Gaza. but the bombs, the drones, the 60,000+ murdered (drastic
undercount) in cold blood wasn't enough for them to speak up?

do you know why the media is finally speaking up about the
6enocide now that there's forced starvation in Gaza? it's because
killing over 60,000 civilians with bombs is called "WAR". but
starving people to death is called wrong, evil, and intentional.
"Israel" was winning the PR war in mainstream media, but now
even mainstream media is beginning to question what's
happening in Gaza…as if they didn't already know. just an FYI
"Israel" has had Gaza on a diet for over 20 years. they've been
killing Gaza slowly for decades…they just needed a big enough
reason to finally 6enocide with the public's approval.

if you've ever felt overworked and underpaid, and have yet to find an escape from this vicious cycle, just know, the U.S. and "Israel" are using your tax dollars to kill children overseas in other countries, instead of spending it on public services and programs to enrich the lives of U.S. citizens. they may not whip people into working harder anymore, but if you stop working you go hungry, you get depressed, you lose the roof over yours and your family's heads, your dreams of buying a nice car become more impossible, and your self-worth diminishes because this is the life we've all accepted as our default, and without it we start to feel futile like our lives serve no purpose. and it's not that it's a complete failure of a system (maybe it is), it's the greed in which our chosen leaders have found ways to make themselves richer off the backs of the working to lower classed citizens. and the idea of classism should give you an automatic sense of unnervingness, and a drive to dismantle it. so as we watch "Israel" 6enocide **Gaza, Palestine**, think about how rich "Israel" gets by stealing more of their land, and how they'll make the U.S. their money back over time by turning Gaza into a "riviera". your perception of "war" and "conflict" is not the same as the people who actually benefit from it. sure, at the end of the day U.S. citizens benefit from war too, because the stolen resources are sold to you in the forms of iPhones, televisions, laptops, your dream car, wedding rings, and even crops. there might be someone reading this who is onboard for this type of modern day slavery in order to sustain a luxury way of living. but nothing about land theft and murder is sustainable…only for the **SHAREHOLDERS**.

P.S. "Israel" also uses U.S. tax dollars to fund their social programs…you know, the one's our billionaire funded government tells us is bad for our economy for us to have basic human rights. to them it's "socialism". but what do you call it when giant corporations go bankrupt and use OUR tax dollars to save their corporation? is that not "socialism" for the rich?

to be Palestinian, you have to forgive your oppressor for murdering your entire family, and for turning your entire neighborhood into a wasteland of concrete slabs and rebar

look the other way and forget that the people who surveil your every move have the right to take your life for simply being Palestinian and wanting to roam freely about the lands of your ancestors steeped harmoniously within the rich history of the soil

not only do they steal your land, they claim your recipes, your art, your culture, and they make it their own, with no one to question their so-called indigenous lifestyle

they are so "Israeli" when they eat "their" hummus, but they are also so "Israeli" when they kill mass amounts of children while the world watches in confusion on whether it's antisemitic to tell them what they're doing is wrong

oh to be more afraid of being labeled antisemitic than to call out the U.S. and "Israel" for committing a 6enocide

your fear and your silence prolongs the mass slaughter happening EVERYDAY since October of 2023

-stop calling it Israel. start calling it Occupied Palestine. if you can't criticize "Israel" #YOURENOTFREE

they're approaching!!
the tanks
the drones
the boots

there's nowhere to hide
the quadcopters know your every move and heartbeat
the search engines, the food we eat, the phones we use, and the
clothes we wear, all of them are in on it
Google, Apple, Puma, Reebok, Louis Vuitton, Microsoft, Meta,
Nestle, McDonalds, Zara…
no one is innocent

what will happen to me in the next few hours is not a movie
you've seen the images
the shredded bodies of children
the slain who were sitting drinking coffee
the mothers walking in the middle of the street holding all
belongings in a bouquet of garbage bags, pulling their child
along, looking for safety but safety means being blown to pieces
anyway

what will happen to me in a few seconds
they're approaching!!
it doesn't matter if i cry for help now
there's nothing you can do to stop them
they've already made up their mind about me
i'm just an animal they can kill with your permission
i'm just a number to you and to them
count me out
689,051

nothing else matters
when you've witnessed a livestreamed 6enocide
nothing else matters

you can never go back to a "regular" life

your favorite diet soda brand, funds the bullet made for the
sniper trained to kill children
the place that sells your favorite cake, is now owned by a
mega-corporation open about its support for "Israel" to murder
children in Gaza
all your favorite athletes who are millionaires, are still dribbling
balls, swinging bats, and playing defense without ever saying a
word about the thousands of children being killed by "Israel"
(afraid to lose their job and be poor again because Zionists pay
for their extravagant lifestyles. or they're just spineless jocks and
you're their cheerleaders)

nothing else matters
your job feels more and more pointless bagging groceries,
mixing cocktails, getting yelled at because the customers burger
was medium and not RARE, so the food gets tossed in the
garbage, and all you can think about is how "Israel" has been
forcibly starving Palestinians and their children to death for 8
months and counting…

- your idols don't care about you and neither does your job

every time "Israel" bombs a tent, a hospital, a school, a house, a cafe, a car, an ambulance, or a playground, their excuse is that Hamas was in the vicinity. then we find out it was unarmed children clutched to their dolls and their parents, or patients in the hospital seeking cancer treatment, or wounded from shrapnel and pulled from the rubble…babies in incubators! "Israel" has been lying about murdering Palestinians for 77 years and getting away with it. but the majority of the world only started counting "Israel's" crimes on October 7, 2023.

- **sociopath?** or so in love you believe them?

i was born in 1989
i'm now 36 years old
i was 34 when i learned about the Nakba of 1948
what in the actual f*ck were we being taught in school this entire
time? 18 years of historical propaganda
of course our education system teaches us that the white man is
pure, and America is perfect
that our presidents were Gods
they teach us how to spin a dreidel
while indirectly teaching us how to hate Arab Muslims (this
includes stereotyping Indian people as Arab Muslim)
and that the only oppressed people in this world or country are
either Black, or Jewish
both have suffered for different reasons
but only one is still suffering for racism that still exists
the other is having their religion misused as a tool to oppress and
6enocide an entire population of people in Gaza, Palestine, and
the West Bank for the last 77 years. misused covertly by Zionist
Jews, and backed by Zionist "leaders" in high places (the U.S.).

- sorry i'm late, but i'm here now, and all are welcome to speak
up against 6enocide if you genuinely mean it (clout chasers do
exist even in gross times like this)

thank you for reading! now grab a pen, a crayon, a feather, or whatever you use to write with, and please take a moment to write a thought, a prayer, shed a tear, or draw a picture below that you wish to express to the Alaydi family or for Palestine (this space is for you)

what i've learned about Palestinians
they're all dreamers
maybe it's out of necessity or survival?
forced to use their imaginations
forced to dream about freedom
wanting nothing but safety and love for all people including the
people who torture them and steal their land
because of them i'm learning how to turn pain into triumph
the way they take the sound of "Israel's" drones buzzing over
their heads morning, day, and night
and reconstruct them into songs

what i've learned about the Zionists of "Israel"
they're all f*cking psychopaths
and it's irreversible, their indoctrination
are we supposed to forgive them when they ask for sympathy?
will their apologies be genuine after they've all smiled on videos,
at the thought of Palestinian children being blown to shreds for
the last 23 months?
the only reason they're protesting against their extremist
government is to avoid damaging their image, and to get a
hostage exchange. they only care about optics.
otherwise, keep murdering!

- *well i guess since you said sorry, you can keep our land now. that's all*
we were looking for was an apology once you're done 6enociding us.
please apologize to my 200 family members you just murdered and
we'll call it even.

Palestinians in Gaza
have become target practice and
test subjects for new weapons
technology. the IOF is treating their
everyday massacres of Palestinians
like a video game. they tell the
media, "no one is innocent in Gaza,
including their offspring" (and we
shrug and do nothing about it).

Gaza Health Ministry reports that the death toll of Palestinians in Gaza since October 7, 2023 is over 64,500 killed by their illegal occupier, "Isreal". **but other reports claim the death toll could be more than half a million**.

i hate using **20,000** to count the slaughter of Palestinian children, knowing it's much, much higher, and that one child killed is one too many.

ONE MORE THING…

if you're donating $100 then spending hundreds more on companies and brands that contribute to the 6enocide, what was even the point?

sure, you fed one family for MAYBE one week.
but all the money you continue to spend on brands that fund the "Israeli" Occupation Forces, and the lifestyles of "Israel's" society eating at fancy restaurants just miles away from the concentration camps where their military and rabid settlers are forcibly starving Gaza and blocking aid, more than cancels out the money you donated a year ago.

this isn't something you just throw $5 at then run to tell your friends how much you support Gaza. it takes actual work and commitment to save the people that are still alive. and furthermore, honoring the martyrs who have been reduced to numbers instead of names, futures, and lovers.

if you still wanna have fun, that's on you. but while you're out having fun, dozens of Palestinians are being killed almost every hour. if you're splurging every week dining out, buying groceries, celebrating birthdays, then you've convinced yourself there's nothing you can do to save Gaza, before you ever even tried. go ahead, exercise your privilege…but don't be chanting FREE PALESTINE at a concert that costs you $400 to attend.

DO BETTER.

companies to boycott (there are plenty of alternatives to these companies and all it takes is a little commitment to make a big enough impact to hurt their bottom lines. we've been raised on these brands and they all run a **monopoly** so it won't be easy but who am i to tell you to do the right thing?)

- Disney
- Coca-Cola
- Apple
- Nestle
- Amazon
- Google
- airbnb
- Chevron
- Microsoft
- Pizza Hut
- McDonalds
- Starbucks
- LVMH brands (Sephora, Louis Vuitton, Tiffany & Co., Dior, Fenty Beauty, etc.)
- Booking.com
- Sodastream
- Burger King
- RE/MAX
- DELL
- INTEL
- Expedia
- Papa Johns
- WiX
- Reebok
- Texaco
- Hyundai

1.
it was never about the hostages
it was always about a land grab, ethnic cleansing, and the
extermination of Palestinians

- headlines by real journalists

2.
i finished writing this book on the day of **September 11, 2025**
the anniversary of some event that happened on stolen land
where people were found mysteriously dead (also the day after the
white-supremacist-conservative-republican-hate-speech-YouTube-influ
encer **Karlie Chirk** was found mysteriously dead)

- headlines in mainstream media owned by Zionists

keywords:
#dehumanization #normalization #saddism #stopgenocide
#zionist #nakba #gaza #palestine #westbank #holocaust
#fuckisrael #gazaholocaust #fuckjizzrael #fuckisrahell
#neveragainmeansneveragainforeveryone #sixisfor6enocide

if you're going to dream
dream for those whose dreams were taken from them
if you're going to the gym
workout as if using your entire soul to lift massive blocks of
rubble off of little children buried below
if you're going to the grocery store
take what you need, then find someone on the streets or in Gaza
to give the rest to
if you need a treat because you're feeling depressed, buy your
treat then donate the same amount you spent on that treat to a
child in Gaza
if you're going to work
remember that your taxes fund "Israel's" 6enocide in Gaza
if you're celebrating birthdays
remember that over 1,000 babies in Gaza were murdered before
the age of 1
if you're going on social media
realize that you're on the other side of the wall, knowingly
having a good laugh while Palestinians in Gaza scream for help.
did you hear something?

- everything we choose to ignore is still connected. do you ever wonder
why philanthropy and charities exist? who creates the need for these
organizations?

there's irony to having a jam-packed refrigerator then still going out for dinner or bringing home bags of takeout.

and those bags of takeout become leftovers most times. leftovers you have no intention of eating in the future but let rot in your refrigerator anyway.

we all do it.

we all want to feel like we're saving the Earth by not being wasteful for once.

it's part of our American tradition.

feasting until we pass out.

wiping our hands from all the hard work at days end so that we can reward ourselves a Hulked-out burrito wrapped in silver armor, a box of fancy Japanese donuts, sushi rolls, **Crumbl** cookies, **Dubai chocolate**, THE WHOLE FUCKING NINE YARDS OF THE AMERICAN VALUE MEAL just to watch your entire list of groceries decay every hour you open your refrigerator looking for anything that wasn't made by God's green Earth.

all that just to say, Gaza is being starved to death by "Israel".

- label your cookies "vegetables" and you'll starve yourself to death won't ya?

SIX is for October **6**th
and all the days before it
that "Israel" has murdered Palestinian land
and people for the last SEVENTY SEVEN years

Labib Dumaidi was a 19-year-old Palestinian boy who was
killed on October 6, 2023 by "Israeli" forces helping "Israeli"
settlers vandalize and attack neighborhoods in the West Bank,
Palestine. settlers taking their usual stroll to harass and steal
more Palestinian land with the backing of military forces
shooting tear gas at families, while simultaneously allowing
settlers to arm themselves against defenseless Palestinian people
minding their own fucking business. this is the role of "Israel".
they are worse than a migraine that goes away for a day, but
comes back each and every day more rabid and foaming at the
mouth, provoking the Palestinian to give the settler a reason to
kill while their military watches or executes the plan for them.
28,105 days of settler violence and military occupation to kill
Palestinians with whatever excuse and made up reason they wish
(all with impunity from the white supremacist world we live in).

- THEY HAVE NAMES

shout out, **Mo Sati**, a Palestinian poet, playwright, and artist from the Bay Area for his
masterful play titled, **THEY HAVE NAMES**. to be Palestinian you have to keep
reminding the world that you're not a number. the day you stop reminding them, is the
day "Israel" exterminates all of Palestine without the world knowing. and the U.S. will
keep the 6enocide of Palestine an even stronger secret than **the Epstein files.**

SOME THINGS ARE BETTER TOLD BY THE ONES LIVING IT

"I can't take this anymore. The genocide is back worse than before. Death is everywhere. My family is trapped, living every second in fear. I've lost friends, neighbors. Sometimes, I wonder if I'll wake up tomorrow? Or if I'll just be another body buried under rubble."
- **Salem Alaydi** (after "Israel" unilaterally broke the ceasefire deal on March 18, 2025)

"Our home was destroyed (along with our schools, and hospitals and all of Gaza). We've been displaced many times. Life became hard, and all my dreams vanished like smoke."
- **Amna Alaydi** (Gofundme Bio)

"There are Palestinian surgeons in Gaza who have seen the bodies of their entire family brought into their hospital, all dead."
- **Dr. Feroze Sidhwa** (trauma surgeon from America working in Gaza)

"Israeli soldiers tell doctors arriving from other countries into Gaza that they cannot bring in medical equipment or baby formula. They confiscate them at checkpoints."
- Dr. Feroze Sidhwa (**forced starvation** in Gaza)

"The other day I asked Keenan, what birds do you know? He said F-35, F-16, Apache, and drone."
- a text message from Dr. Feroze's friend **Nizar** in Gaza asking his **5-year-old** son what kind of birds he knows

"

NOBODY'S FREE UNTIL EVERYBODY'S FREE

- Fannie Lou Hamer

FREE PALESTINE
FREE CONGO
FREE SUDAN
FREE SYRIA
FREE LEBANON
FREE TIGRAY
FREE HAITI
FREE HAWAII
FREE PUERTO RICO
FREE GUAM
FREE ALL OPPRESSED PEOPLE
AND **FUCK ICE**
https://www.ccijustice.org/carrn

About the Author

daniel s. reyes is a writer, artist, and relentless truth-teller. his work moves between poetry, reflection, and social critique, always rooted in a commitment to justice and the preservation of memory. writing from the intersections of personal witness and collective struggle, reyes refuses to sanitize reality, instead choosing language that challenges, unsettles, and provokes. "SIX is for 6enocide" is his latest offering, a testament to the belief that words can resist annihilation, amplify silenced voices, and demand that the world pay attention.

Authors Note

I cannot stress enough how important it is to speak up and be on the right side of history. What we're seeing from our world leaders is their complete whitewash denial of the genocide "Israel" is committing in Gaza. None of it is justified. How are they allowed to ship stockpiles of bombs and highly sophisticated weapons to "Israel" by the BILLION$, then gaslight the public saying, "Hamas is lying about the death toll in Gaza"? But we see the slaughter on our phones. And the most credible human rights organizations, and doctors from around the globe who have treated in Gaza are telling us *all day long* they see death entering their hospitals, and the hospital facilities are always in a constant rattle by "Israel's" bombs. Oh, and **Ms. Rachel for Littles** is "Hamas", according to "Israel". I want you to know this book isn't about me. This book is about trying to wake the world. Trying to reach your heart for Palestine. To get you to slowly stop your routine. Focus on the genocide. The world is burning in our silence and inaction. Start a fast from your regular day. This is bigger than you and me, but collectively every little effort counts. Start to track how wasteful of a person you are and the people around you, in comparison to Palestinian lives being forced to drink contaminated water, eat rotted food off the ground, sift through maggot infested flour, sit in the stench of death and low sanitation, watch their newborn die slow and painful because the mother is malnourished and has limited access to food and water and no baby formula. I could keep going, but I want you to take this book seriously, as a push. If you're reading this, you now have no excuse to ignore the genocide. ALL EYES ON GAZA, PALESTINE. *For the Alaydi family, with love* 🩶

unfortunately you can't make a living during a genocide so please donate, we're their only source of funds.

ALL I WANTED TO DO WAS CELEBRATE LIFE AND BE FREE
BUT WHEN THE WORLD STAYS SILENT ABOUT THINGS THAT MATTER
IT FORCES THE REST OF US TO FREE THOSE WHO DONT EVEN
KNOW THEY'RE NOT FREE.